To Cut

To Cutting Me Open, and Spilling Me Out

By: n.s. burton

To Cutting Me Open, and Spilling Me Out

To Cutting Me Open, and Spilling Me Out

TABLE OF CONTENTS

SHATTERED 11-38

IN RECOVERY 39-74

TO SECOND CHANCES 75-100

SHE FINDS LOVE AGAIN 101-127

To Cutting Me Open, and Spilling Me Out

To Cutting Me Open, and Spilling Me Out

TRIGGER WARNING:

this collection discusses themes of:
Depression
Anxiety
Suicidal Ideation
Self-harm

To Cutting Me Open, and Spilling Me Out

To Cutting Me Open, and Spilling Me Out

Dedication:

This is for the ones who have been ripped into too many pieces to count and too many to put it back together. For the ones who understand relapse. This is for the ones who hate recovery but pray for it. So that they no longer need to feel this pain. For the ones who chose to love their scars no matter how deep or how visible they are to the eyes of the ones that don't understand. And finally to those of us who have been able to love again.

To Cutting Me Open, and Spilling Me Out

To Cutting Me Open, and Spilling Me Out

To Cutting Me Open, and Spilling Me Out

by n.s. burton

To Cutting Me Open, and Spilling Me Out

To Cutting Me Open, and Spilling Me Out

SHATTERED

To Cutting Me Open, and Spilling Me Out

Death has consumed
my life
It's trying to

consume me;
I think
it's winning

To Cutting Me Open, and Spilling Me Out

You Linger Inside Still

As I remember
my chest collapsed.

the way you once
held me up to
show me
off to the world
telling them
that I was
yours

the way you
once grabbed

my waist and kissed
me until we were
taking each
other's air

the way your arms
wrapped themselves
around my
tiny figure to
protect me from

To Cutting Me Open, and Spilling Me Out

the world
around us
the way you
once told me, marrying
me was
what God created
you for
missing you
causes the hole
in my stomach to
fall into itself growing
until my insides
are no more. Until I have
emptied everything
out of me.
Where I am nothing but bones
with no flesh
No heart
and no soul

No life yet to
give or to
take
missing you is
the worst
thing I can do

To Cutting Me Open, and Spilling Me Out

May 5

"We shouldn't have gotten back together so soon"
"I was lonely"
"I'm not breaking up with you"
"I'm not happy"

"I don't know what do to anymore"
"I don't feel like I'm in love"
     "Cold feet?"
"Something like that"

7 reasons to cut. 7 reasons I want to.

     7 reasons to scream.
     7 reasons I hate
     7 reasons to do it,
          and not 1 reason to not.

To Cutting Me Open, and Spilling Me Out

1:58am

breathe, but then

    I wonder

what would

happen
    if

        I

            just

        stopped.

To Cutting Me Open, and Spilling Me Out

Late Night Means You

I now wonder how
long the cuts
on my hips
will be bleeding him—

out of me.

To Cutting Me Open, and Spilling Me Out

July 23

I hoped you'd find me,
but you never did

I wasn't yours
to find anymore

To Cutting Me Open, and Spilling Me Out

Idolizing

You grow up being
told that you should
never idolize someone,
it's bad they said.

But they also told you that
drinking and
swearing are bad.

Yet they swear like a sailor
and drink like alcoholics

And so, I idolize you
because you are
perfect,
despite the pain—
regardless of the
passing time

To Cutting Me Open, and Spilling Me Out

Love— Hell

Love is beautiful.
I would know, I got lost in it.
Love is challenging
I would know, I've seen the obstacles.
Love is mysterious,
I would know, I got stabbed by it.

Love is hell
I would know,
        I'm still here

To Cutting Me Open, and Spilling Me Out

Sept 3

I miss him,
apart of me knows
I would choose to die

if I had to pick life or to
hear him say
'I love you' one
more time
Before closing
my eyes for
the last time

To Cutting Me Open, and Spilling Me Out

A Garden Full

They like to call her, Flower
pick her up and watch her slowly die
They like to call her, Flower
to admire her beauty

but as the days go by
it begins to fade
they like to call her, Flower
and slowly watch her die
for they have a garden filled
with Flowers

To Cutting Me Open, and Spilling Me Out

self harm
is such an easy
lifestyle. The edge
of the blade
catching against
my brown skin
Relief floods
through me, as
blood escapes me.

To Cutting Me Open, and Spilling Me Out

It is all the same really

Welcoming back the old habits
is like taking back that
asshole ex
because all it does
is hurt you in the end.
But it feels so good
at first.

So with that,
I open my arms
as I watch
him make
his way to me.
I take a moment to
take him in…

To Cutting Me Open, and Spilling Me Out

His hair is perfectly brushed
one hair out of place,
his faded blue jeans hang just low enough
for the tip of his grey boxers
to show when his black shirt lifts up.

He is as breathtaking
as I remember,
I am speechless
when embracing him.
He smells exactly
like I remember.
                …and the blade
feels just as I remember.

To Cutting Me Open, and Spilling Me Out

the anger inside

I have this anger that lies in me deep down.
Its been there for a while, but I'm not sure where it came from.
Who built the fire inside me and let it grow without containing it
When did I become angry inside?

I used to be happy,
I knew nothing but happiness, but here I stand in the middle
of my anger surrounded
by flames
waiting to burn

To Cutting Me Open, and Spilling Me Out

Sept. 21

Our skin is such
a fragile thing. Its like God
is testing us. Don't
hurt it.
But its fragile ness
makes pain an
easy access.

I love the
color of blood.
The way it stains
my clothes
at night.
The way it shines
under the florescent bathroom
light. Down my body
dripping from my

thin to the title floor.

I am the
canvas. This blood
my paint coated on my bladed paintbrush

To Cutting Me Open, and Spilling Me Out

Being an addict is quite easy
I understand why many people refuse to stop
Why stop if its the only thing comforting you
I mean, why turn your back away
from the one thing that you have left
I'm an addict and
I'm completely fine with it

To Cutting Me Open, and Spilling Me Out

My cry for help

How is it that nobody see the slits on my wrist
or the ones on my hips
doesn't matter how hard I scream
the destruction I make
nobody hears a thing
I am just a girl who does
nothing but bleeds

To Cutting Me Open, and Spilling Me Out

11:47am

Why is it
that love is
something
so precious
yet so
damaging?
Love can
hold you
up right.

But it's ca-
pable
of disman-
tling. Burn-
ing you.
The
power it
has over us
is
deadly.

To Cutting Me Open, and Spilling Me Out

But if this
is true why
am I
searching

for some-
one that
has

      al-
ready

killed me?

To Cutting Me Open, and Spilling Me Out

I feel like there is something inside of me—
something wrong
that's eating me inside out
and that one day
its going to win
and that will be the only thing remaining

To Cutting Me Open, and Spilling Me Out

Continue

I have loved once in my life time and I know that it is rare and wonderful. I want nothing more than to have you hold me in your arms once more. To have your cold lips touch my brown skin. To cherish the way you way you whispered "I love you" while I closed my eyes and fell asleep to your heart beat.
How I tried to match your breathing so that we can become one. How I wanted nothing more than to be yours for the rest of my life. But now all I want is to share our love with the world. To let them learn that heartbreak and pain is there to catch you if you aren't careful.

To Cutting Me Open, and Spilling Me Out

Old habits

One must remember
that old habits die hard.
And weak people
fall more than those
who have the confidence
and power to fight back.
I must remember
that old habits die hard
and that I am a weak person

who has no energy
to fight back.
And so I fall back into
the habit that is so comforting
and the only thing
that was there for
me all those months ago.
             Day 1

To Cutting Me Open, and Spilling Me Out

The last good thing you said to me

"You're my Christmas"

12. 25
11:20pm

To Cutting Me Open, and Spilling Me Out

June 19

You wanted to hurt me that day. I remember it. We met at the dollar tree down the street from my place. I was happy that day. Bubbly. The girl you remembered falling in love with back in high school. It confused you. Why was I capable of being this happy when a few days ago I was crying in your car after you told me you wanted a break? Was it possible that I was happy not being yours? I left without a hug. You called me back. I gave you a side pat on the back, you wouldn't have it. You hugged me tight. Made sure I could feel your heart beating in my chest. You wanted me to break. How I should have seen it. How cruel you were. The capability you had of hurting me just in order to make sure I wasn't happy without you.

To Cutting Me Open, and Spilling Me Out

You ruined Christmas.

To Cutting Me Open, and Spilling Me Out

To Cutting Me Open, and Spilling Me Out

IN RECOVERY

To Cutting Me Open, and Spilling Me Out

Sept 3

It's the wildfire you
should fear
for its beauty is too great—
but its pain that kills you
that burns deep
are unfelt
until it's done
it's job.

To Cutting Me Open, and Spilling Me Out

11:59 p.m

progress is being able to
read the words
written months ago

and no longer
feeling the anger

To Cutting Me Open, and Spilling Me Out

satan looked a lot like
you. and

a lot like
me. sin
was our home

To Cutting Me Open, and Spilling Me Out

12:24 a.m

I wonder if you were aware of all the sins
you were creating in me
or if I was just someone
to risk

someone who was good for you
to use for all the wrong reasons
but all the right ways
it's funny
no matter how much time has passed
when I look for inspiration
I think of you

To Cutting Me Open, and Spilling Me Out

Hi
I miss you—
I'm allowed to
I'm allowed to be sad
10 months is nothing
10 months hurts like a *bitch*

I hate you. I loved you. I miss you.
I can't remember how

your skin felt
against mine
        anymore…

To Cutting Me Open, and Spilling Me Out

12:50pm

Getting better sounds a lot like spilling your secrets to people who pretend to care
Everyone needs to just back the fuck off.
If I don't feel like eating three fucking meals a day why the fuck do you care.
If I don't feel like weighing more than 115 that's my fucking choice.
This is my body I get to do whatever the fuck I want to it.

To Cutting Me Open, and Spilling Me Out

I don't want to fucking die so everyone needs to just back off.
I don't want to kill myself so everyone needs to just shut up.
I don't care.
I don't give a shit.
I want to do what I want to do.
I want to not eat.
I want to go to school and work.
If I want to use a fucking razor that's on me

not them.
everyone just need to mind their own fucking business.

I want everyone to stop giving a shit
and just go about their issues.

Just leave me the fuck alone.
       It's raw, and dark, but it's me.
It was us.
              It's what is left of me.

To Cutting Me Open, and Spilling Me Out

Feb. 19

I am stronger than the bad
I am stronger than the emptiness that is inside of me
I am not too broken I can be enough
without you
I can be enough
I can be enough.
I will fix myself

To Cutting Me Open, and Spilling Me Out

Love is cruel
it hurts destroys
everything inside me
No one will fill the hole
you left
Because no one
will be able to find
what is left of
me.

To Cutting Me Open, and Spilling Me Out

I now wonder how
long I will be bleeding
your name. How many more times
my pens will
scribble down your
name.

Perhaps until
the end of time
Despite the months
that have
passed and the boys
I've kissed. My pen continues
to spill
kissing your name with
its ballpoint tip

To Cutting Me Open, and Spilling Me Out

Your name was once
the thing that gave me breathe
it was
my oxygen
now,
all it does it cause me to drown
in emptiness

I am not pure you are
not whole you are poison
and I drank it up
like a cup
of tea

To Cutting Me Open, and Spilling Me Out

I'm not perfect.
I'm flawed
I'm unloveable
I'm a mess

Broken, damaged.
Not enough, never enough

I am only
damaged

To Cutting Me Open, and Spilling Me Out

belonging to you

I've decided today, to move on
and forget about you.
To learn and erase you from my
memory as if it will be easy as 1,2,3
and A B C
I decided today was the day I got my life back
But then I realize my life was not mine to decide
such things, it was always yours.
how silly me for thinking otherwise

To Cutting Me Open, and Spilling Me Out

2:41pm

Recovery does not always
mean moving forward
Not always smiling
day after day
It is
forgiving. crying
about the loss
it is about being gentle.

To Cutting Me Open, and Spilling Me Out

Sometimes
I want to drown
the water
is so blue
crystal blue
a magic
takes over
its called
      Depression.
                            Frustration
              Confusion.
sometimes
I feel like
the sting of
the blade is
better then
the feeling
of running my fingers
over my hips

to find no cut
no gaps
no bloody bandaids
no red stained
tissue in the
toilet

To Cutting Me Open, and Spilling Me Out

Please know
I am
          dying...

no

trying.

To Cutting Me Open, and Spilling Me Out

I cannot understand why you will not just leave me alone.
why must you push your life to collide with mine?
You left my life. You did not want to be in it
You left
So please. Stay gone

To Cutting Me Open, and Spilling Me Out

I'm pretty sure the universe hates me
Because it made me a hopeless romantic. Obsessed with
literature
and took the only boy I loved away
now watching two people love each other
pulls at
my insides
that hold me together
it loosens them, and
I'm pretty sure I'll fall
        apart
any moment

To Cutting Me Open, and Spilling Me Out

There is something
inside of me that
refuses to breath correctly
and I'm not sure why

To Cutting Me Open, and Spilling Me Out

6:12pm

I loved the way I ran,
until every bone in my body broke
I ran and ran and ran
loved loved and loved
perfected my form and practiced for hours
memorizing his perfections
and movements for days on end

Running was what I thought I was born to do
as I thought I was meant to love him forever
I ran the same way I loved
Until I was out of breath and my limbs were fractured
until it was too much and his love broke
Running was all I knew and so was he

    So what now?

To Cutting Me Open, and Spilling Me Out

Death calls
for me
at all
hours.

But
at 3am
        he lingers
        the
                l o n g e s t .

To Cutting Me Open, and Spilling Me Out

10:59pm

I hope
it was not
easy to walk
away as you
thought
it could be

I hope
every Justin Bieber song
you hear you
think of me.
Every time
Taylor Swift comes on

you sing along.

To Cutting Me Open, and Spilling Me Out

Sometimes I wonder if I keep choosing the wrong path.
And destiny is royally pissed at me for not listening to her in the first place.
Or if fate is disappointed at me for rebelling.
Perhaps, I'm making all these mistakes and forgiving all the wrong people.
At a young age people tell you life is hard.
But you never truly believe it because you hope to get the golden ticket.
I am not a perfect human being.
I have scars and flaws and I make a lot of mistakes.
But despite all that, I have still chosen to stay.
And I hope destiny and fate are proud of that.

To Cutting Me Open, and Spilling Me Out

sometimes I forget how much power
I have over my own body.
how easy it would be to
end my own life.
how something as simple
as taking a bottle of pills or
grabbing a knife;
       could just end it.
scary how much power
I have over my own
body. how I can manage to force
myself to starve all day.
that being nothing is better
than being full— with nothing
      so much power.
             but so much weakness as well

To Cutting Me Open, and Spilling Me Out

December 5

It's been over a year and six months since I've see you.
Since I've talked to you.
It's been six months since I have had the need to text you
and call you.
My anxiety is high
My mom is busy
And the only person I feel like would help me

Breath
It out
Is you

To Cutting Me Open, and Spilling Me Out

2:36pm

You do not care
Or think about me
But I care
And think about
You.
I wish we could be like before
Where I would
Be on the bathroom floor
Crying
And your voice would come
through the speaker of
my phone
Telling me to breath
I miss the way your
Voice calmingly said I love you
And made sure to remind me that
you'll be there
To pick me up.

To Cutting Me Open, and Spilling Me Out

Public Restroom

Sometimes I let my depression win and let it walk me into the public restroom and not leave for an hour. Anxiety stays. Lingers in the dark corner inside of you. It rests itself. Breathes you in, memorizing every part that is in you. Remember the fears that the world has planted in you. So when it comes it's on fire. Burning the inside of your organs. Putting flames on your lungs. Making it impossible to breath correctly. The mind is screaming. But words cannot come up or out when the rest of your body is a heat of light oranges and reds giving you burns. Every part is so tender there is nothing safe anymore. You are burning down into the anxiety. He now owns you. You are nothing more than silence— the scream that cannot be heard

To Cutting Me Open, and Spilling Me Out

August 22,

It's been a year and three months. And I find myself remembering you
Waiting for me outside of class
Every day.
With the grey jacket on that I bought you for Christmas a year go.
With your head buried in your phone— playing your favorite game of the month.
As I close my eyes, I can see everything so clear.
I can feel my heart racing.
My smile beaming.
I was so in love with you. I thought I would away be so in love with you
but oh, how wrong I was.

To Cutting Me Open, and Spilling Me Out

11:47am

We're all fucked after this aren't we?
It's all doctors appointments.
Psychiatric appointments.
Therapy. And more therapy.
And then group therapy.
No such thing as normal once you've had it

Maybe that's what I hate about you the most.
That you did this to me.
You gave me this illness and now
I am screwed

To Cutting Me Open, and Spilling Me Out

Innocence

Because being kissed by
a sweet boy who
wants to know the way your brain
works and the books you've memorized
will always be
the purest things I know

To Cutting Me Open, and Spilling Me Out

It's all about a girl who loses herself in more ways than one,
but ends up finding herself
    a little along the away

To Cutting Me Open, and Spilling Me Out

I am
enough words

To Cutting Me Open, and Spilling Me Out

The scars on my body
are only pain that me
and my therapist know

To Cutting Me Open, and Spilling Me Out

Recovery will forever be an on going battle. It is not a once in a life time process. Recovery will always be in my life. I will always want to relapse and find myself drowning all over again. But now I have the tools to get myself through the water to make it to the surface without cutting. Recovery is about being vulnerable, always.

You, are not alone.

To Cutting Me Open, and Spilling Me Out

To Cutting Me Open, and Spilling Me Out

TO SECOND CHANCES

To Cutting Me Open, and Spilling Me Out

No date

I am happy.
      I am alive.
           I am beautiful.

To Cutting Me Open, and Spilling Me Out

A year
and a half
of pain
I have made
it this
far. alive
and breathing

To Cutting Me Open, and Spilling Me Out

Death is not
okay.

Stop.

                Be here.

To Cutting Me Open, and Spilling Me Out

recovery is painful
and a forever
on going process

To Cutting Me Open, and Spilling Me Out

Fuck you
and your
apology. I
don't want
it. I don't
deserve
this. I am
happy.
Time has
passed, it
is too late
for you to
come back
and say
you are
sorry. I am
happy. Do
not come
and think
that
I will let

To Cutting Me Open, and Spilling Me Out

you back in
because
you are
wrong. I
am not the
same girl
you left in
the parking
lot
years ago. I
am no
longer
weak and
need a boy
to feel
whole
again.
I am free.
So fuck
your apol-
ogy. I don't
need it
anymore.

To Cutting Me Open, and Spilling Me Out

it's moments like
this where I
learned it's okay
    to be alone.

    Even when he
        wants to

                hold me.

To Cutting Me Open, and Spilling Me Out

Happy February,
I am happy

      I love

myself.

To Cutting Me Open, and Spilling Me Out

that's always the start.

To Cutting Me Open, and Spilling Me Out

I always thought I talked too much.
Told him too much.
My thoughts became every word out of my mouth.
No secrets. Just pain.
Lots of it
I talked and talked. Never shut up about how I am never enough for him.
For you.
I was all words that surrounded us so much— too much.
But. In the quiet.
When you walked away.
I realized. It's not that I talked too much.
It's that you never talked.
I was the perfect amount of words.
I was enough words.
You just weren't the one who was supposed to be listening

To Cutting Me Open, and Spilling Me Out

The day I was able to use a razor
and not self harm was the day I knew
I would be okay.
But it will always
be my enemy. Despite how many
years pass by. My body will

be my enemy the way it starts to
grow in unknown places. My mind does
not know how to take care
of my body. So I ignore my mind
and let me body do it's job

To Cutting Me Open, and Spilling Me Out

No Date

Its the ones that keep you up all night writing you need to worry about

To Cutting Me Open, and Spilling Me Out

To the ones who
inspire me
to write,

To Cutting Me Open, and Spilling Me Out

feelings are
real. they say that
they are rare.
to acknowledge
them.
my feelings
are beautiful
you are
too— your mind
is a garden
thorns and lilies
in the same
garden.
      and my feels
      for your garden
      are strong
      There is love
      at night
      and during the
      day when the sun
      is shining and the
      moon is vibrating
      within the stars.
      love is rare.
      acknowledge it

To Cutting Me Open, and Spilling Me Out

untitled

Please note that I fear commitment because I'm always the one left behind.
I am never the one to walk away.
Thats how all of this started because I told myself that I don't want to commit.
But the problem is, what if I do? What happens then?
    To be healthy again,
Maybe you're what I've been wanting
I think you're healthy for me.
I'm not one to usually want healthy things.
But when it comes to you, it's nice and refreshing.
Like the first day of summer, when the sun is beaming and the world is at peace with itself.
I feel relaxed around you like I can be myself.
Not having to try so hard, I can breathe around you.
Maybe I'm finally done hurting myself, maybe I'm ready to be healthy again.
Because a few weeks ago I was able to stare at myself in the mirror and tell myself "I am good enough" and "i'm a good person."
Because as much as it's hard to admit it, loving myself is the first step.
And after a year I finally made that step
Maybe you're my second

To Cutting Me Open, and Spilling Me Out

8:56pm

I sit here.
Across from you.
For the first time in years.
All the questions answered
the second you walked in
It was 6 o'clock on a Monday
Night. I watched you through
The corner of my eye starring
At me.

You called me, "the
One that got away"

Both suicidal whether on
Accident or on purpose, both.

Now I lay here in
My bed.
Miles away from
You.
Thankful to be done.
Feeling all of the pain
You caused me
Over the years.
My heart
Aches.

To Cutting Me Open, and Spilling Me Out

From happiness and
Pain.
I can breath yet
I can't get enough
Air. I lay still. Trying to remember—

Telling myself I did
Good.
I am in no pain
No hate.
No love for
You anymore. I have moved forward
Moved on.

Breathed new air. New life
New me. New happiness.
And I thank god. For what he did
To me all those years ago.
Because I now love
Myself. Happy with myself.
Depressed some days but no longer
Because of him. No longer cutting
My beautiful caramel brown
Skin. I no longer bang
My head against the wall... floor.
Instead I play it down
On my white cold
Pillow. Grateful
To be alive. To feel
This closure.

To Cutting Me Open, and Spilling Me Out

1:04am

you are strong.
i know this
because last night
all you talked about was dying
but now its tomorrow
and you lay peaceful asleep right beside me

To Cutting Me Open, and Spilling Me Out

Bathtubes

This comfort sheds no blood

To Cutting Me Open, and Spilling Me Out

My world does not
Stop or
End because you stop
Loving me. Because
I still love
Me

To Cutting Me Open, and Spilling Me Out

I

am

A L I V E

To Cutting Me Open, and Spilling Me Out

And to the guy
that broke me
many, many years
ago. This is not for you.

This is for the broken girls,
the recovering ones, the *survivors.*
The ones who didn't believe
they could live without
him, her, they, them…
despite the
fact that they wanted to
die every moment of
the day.
They didn't. They live.

Because in the end.
You are nothing, but
a scared boy who ran.

To Cutting Me Open, and Spilling Me Out

12:32pm

To each one of you.
Thank you for being kind and gentle with me. For allowing me to be a different form of myself and accepting her. For being yourself and learning to trust me with your secrets. Thank you for understanding and making me laugh when I didn't know how to anymore. Most importantly I hope you are beyond happy, and that you found someone to love you and care for you. Someone who makes you want to be a better person everyday. Someone to love and be loved with, to make you smile until your cheeks hurt, laugh until your stomach is about to explode. Because I found my someone, and I hope you find yours too.

To Cutting Me Open, and Spilling Me Out

To Cutting Me Open, and Spilling Me Out

To Cutting Me Open, and Spilling Me Out

SHE FINDS LOVE AGAIN

To Cutting Me Open, and Spilling Me Out

Thank you, for being here at the end
of this chapter.
And not at the beginning.
Because we
now have a
whole book of our
own.

To Cutting Me Open, and Spilling Me Out

The last book store, 3:33pm

I always thought
I would find
my love
in a bookstore
or he would find me. Turns
out the my love is
walking along
side me
in a bookstore. Sharing
my passion for literature
in his own way.

To Cutting Me Open, and Spilling Me Out

11:11pm May 09

You look at
me as if
I am one of a
kind. As though there
aren't other brown
eyed, curly haired
girls roaming around
soaking up the
sunshine streets
of California

As though your lily
pad green eyes have
never matched a pair
of almond brown
before. Your baby
pink lips press against
my forehead to whisper
a secret our lips
have yet to share

To Cutting Me Open, and Spilling Me Out

Unspoken Thoughts

"You know, I think I could love you."
"Oh yeah?"
"Maybe. In another world."
"Why not this one?"
"Because you would already love me if it was going to be this one."
Boy was she wrong.

To Cutting Me Open, and Spilling Me Out

_10:23am_

I think I could love him.
And I can't wait for the day
he loves me. Who would
have known— that love was a
possibility. You're green yellow
Eyes could find the
Beauty in my brown
Ones. I think I can love you.
If you let me.
I hope you will.
Because it would be an honor to

To Cutting Me Open, and Spilling Me Out

January 19. 7:11pm

Happiness runs through his veins
And I can feel it running through mine
He is new and wonderful
I am new and hopeful
Together we are stronger
Individually
He is knowledgeable
I am incredible
He makes this work.
The way I run my hands through the back of his shaved neck.
Sends chills down his thin body
Sends thrill into my tiny one
He is beautiful
And might be mine

To Cutting Me Open, and Spilling Me Out

12:38am

I refers to lose you to a guy who means nothing to me anymore.
I refers to be the reason that you and I do not become an us.
Because
I refers to let someone else control my happiness.
I refers to be sad for the rest of my life. I deserve to be happy.
I might not deserve you but I'm just to try to show you, that I do.

To Cutting Me Open, and Spilling Me Out

January 27

There's something about you.
The way you light up
My day with your presence
How I can stare at you for hours
Never ending
Conversations in the car
Everything about you makes me
Become a better person
I learn from you.
How to care better
To communicate more
Our openness is endless

To Cutting Me Open, and Spilling Me Out

March 12 1:14am

There are three words
Eight letters that
Scare the shit
Out of the world.
When I'm with you
I never thought
I could
Find someone
Who would understand

My pain
Three words
That's all it takes
To give someone
Your heart
Without realizing
You already did

To Cutting Me Open, and Spilling Me Out

D.

The way your hand caresses my neck
Sends energy down my body
While your hand rubs
My cheek
I'm in bliss
You are the sky
I am the ocean
And we have found our coast
The one where we are always
Touching.
Green and blue eyes.
How lucky am I
That I get both just by looking
At you.
1:15pm

To Cutting Me Open, and Spilling Me Out

11:11pm May 09

You look at
me as if
I am one of a
kind. As though there
aren't other brown
eyed, curly haired
girls roaming around
soaking up the
sunshine streets
of California

To Cutting Me Open, and Spilling Me Out

May 27

Leaving a target parking lot
At a stop light
You mumbled
"I love you"

At a red light
I stopped too
Breathing
The world paused
Too. Your face was so sure
Of the words you just breathed out

Into the world
The light turned green
The universe was tell me
To go
With you—
To fall with *you*

To Cutting Me Open, and Spilling Me Out

4:23 August 2

You have yellow in
Your eyes. That matches the
Yellow in my soul

To Cutting Me Open, and Spilling Me Out

Waking up at 3am

Tossing and tuning
In the cold white sheets
Not able to sleep
Racking my brain
To figure out what is
Wrong.

Realizing at 4:19am
That nothing is wrong
But I am in love
With this guy
The one who respects me
And isn't afraid of telling
Me the truth— even if I don't
Want to hear it.
Being in love after the
First break up
After the
First year of depression
And another of recovery
Being in love is

To Cutting Me Open, and Spilling Me Out

Wholesome. It gives my heart
Butterflies. Humming to the
Thought of seeing him
Again. To knowing

He loves me.

I
love
Him.

We are spectacular, we are fireworks
In July. And hot chocolate with
The hint of a candy cane. We are
The free feeling of December 31st
The freshness of January 1st
We are in love— again.

For the first
Time
all over.

To Cutting Me Open, and Spilling Me Out

9:43pm

I hate being in
Love and vulnerable
Because it increases
My chance
Of getting hurt
by you. Because
Love means giving you
A piece of you I
Wasn't prepared to
Give in the first
Place. But I love that
I did. Even though
That means living
in fear of
Being hurt by you

To Cutting Me Open, and Spilling Me Out

There has been a life time of love that I didn't know could develop between two people in such a short amount of them. But here we are. A lifetime of love is what we bring. A love I didn't know I was capable of receiving. Of allowing someone to love me in such a way. I didn't know what was in store for me, while I was sitting in pain for so long. But a lifetime of love is coming for you. Yes you, reading this. No matter where you hurt or have felt. It's going to find you. But first, you must step into the sun.

To Cutting Me Open, and Spilling Me Out

9:28pm

I'm over the moon in love

To Cutting Me Open, and Spilling Me Out

The past may
haunt me at times
but the future
bring me to
the light

To Cutting Me Open, and Spilling Me Out

You
make
me
brave

To Cutting Me Open, and Spilling Me Out

12:16pm

You are
the love I
never had
and the one
I didn't know
I needed

To Cutting Me Open, and Spilling Me Out

12:24am

But falling asleep
in your arms is
the safest I've every felt

To Cutting Me Open, and Spilling Me Out

I sat in the dark for so long
I forgot what the sun felt like
and by *god* is it beautiful

To Cutting Me Open, and Spilling Me Out

10:50pm

I still
get butterflies
when you
kiss me
like *that.*

To Cutting Me Open, and Spilling Me Out

7:39pm

I love the way
you say
my full
name, like you
know every part
of me —
I
think
you might

To Cutting Me Open, and Spilling Me Out

Theres a happiness in my
almond brown eyes
that wasn't there before.
A smile that shows
no faults. No, these
eyes carry light
inside them
now.
when they look
at you— they shine
brighter than the fullest
moon on its
darkest night.

To Cutting Me Open, and Spilling Me Out

To Cutting Me Open, and Spilling Me Out

Dear Past Self,

I want to apologize.
For letting you destroy your body and soul, the way I let you treat us now seems a bit unforgivable. But, i know how much you were hurting... the agony of feeling lost and unwanted. Of doubting ourselves when we desperately needed to believe in us.
I'm sorry, for letting you rip us to pieces, thinking we deserved it. I promise you, you didn't.

But, we made it.

Out of that dark place, with more scars than we went in with... but we made it. And I am damn happy to say we did.

Thank you, for not giving up.

Love,
Future You

To Cutting Me Open, and Spilling Me Out

To Cutting Me Open, and Spilling Me Out

To Cutting Me Open, and Spilling Me Out

ACKNOWLEDGMENTS

Thank you to the readers that decided to pick this book up and look into its raw beauty. For letting these words swallow you whole and hopefully cause you to feel something or perhaps feels something.

I would like to thank all of those who have supported me on this long journey and for never doubting my ability to do it; especially when I did.

First, I would like to thank my best friend, the one who saw all of my darkest moments, my deepest of secrets and scars, yet still decided to walk with me through it all. For saving part of my life.

Second, to Jasmine Darling, for this wouldn't be here without you. You have been my backbone throughout this whole process, making sure to push me and hold my hand when needed. I thank you for our friendship and being my soul sister. Okay?

Third, to my cousin for loving me and my work. For being my hype girl, and for creating the gorgeous girl on my front cover.

Lastly, the most important person in my life. My soulmate, thank you for being the sun that came out after years of darkness. I am forever grateful for us finding our way to each other. For you have *seen*, felt, and mending all of my scars. And loved me through it all, my biggest supporter— without you I would not know true love.

To Cutting Me Open, and Spilling Me Out
ABOUT THE AUTHOR

Nicole Burton is from Los Angeles, California. She graduated from California State University of Long Beach with her B.A in English, Creative Writing and a minor in Sociology. Her passion for reading developed her love for writing (as many readers).
She believes that there's a rawness in writing about your own life experience. In choosing to write about her own, she hopes to let her readers know if they are suffering, they are not alone. Mental health is a daily struggle, and it's okay to be vulnerable— to be heard.
 Find her on Instagram @author.nsburton

To Cutting Me Open, and Spilling Me Out

TO CUTTING ME OPEN, AND SPILLING ME OUT

copyright © 2023 by Nicole Burton.
All rights reserved. No part of this book may be used or reproduced in any way whatsoever without written permission except in the case of reprints in the context of reviews.

ISBN: 9798862606270 (Paperback)

Cover designed by Nicole Burton

Made in the USA
Las Vegas, NV
25 January 2024